Short Notes and Poetry

We're All looking for something...
How many of us know what that is even if we find it?

Randon Thorn

Order this book online at www.trafford.com
or email orders@trafford.com

Most Trafford titles are also available at major online book retailers.

Print information available on the last page.

ISBN: 978-1-4120-6332-6 (sc)
ISBN: 978-1-4269-4142-9 (e)

Trafford rev. 10/16/2018

Trafford
PUBLISHING   www.trafford.com
North America & international
toll-free: 1 888 232 4444 (USA & Canada)
fax: 812 355 4082

Introduction

The following collection of whatever you'd like to call them are all either very enlightening, realistic, funny, serious or sad. Rather mumbo-jumbo style as viewed from either gender's viewpoint as there is really not any set pattern that Love relationships and affairs must follow. As a matter of fact, they are all very unorganized. If you have experienced an organized Love relationship / affair, then you are very fortunate indeed. Don't look for any organization in this book. You won't find it. Just read it.

The style used in this publication is designed to make the reader stop, think and feel. Some of the material comes from the author's first hand experiences. Some comes from who knows where. Any names used which may appear to be a possible association with a real person are not intended and are purely circumstantial or coincidental.

The author feels that you, the reader, should identify with most all of the material used and hopes his work might be of some help in any Love relationship past, present and future. He also wants you to realize a couple of simple things... Nobody's perfect until you fall in Love with them and Love is not Perfect, it's only Love.

Randon

I'm dedicating this book to the next
Love of my life, whoever and wherever she might be . . .

Suzanne _____
I think I'm in
TROUBLE!
Love,
Randon **1986**

We all make mistakes!
Love,
Randon **1987**

I'm actually dedicating this book to my mother.
We ALL have one of those you know.

One summer night back in the 80's my mother and I were talking. I told her that I was writing a book to be published. I told her what it was about and some of the things that were in it. She read one of my poems and started to cry. She said, "I've got something you can use in your book" and she recited these next few words, which I promised her would be published in my book someday. My mother died August 9, 1990 before this book was published, but I've kept my promise. She simply said...

"When you go...
All I know... of life, of Love and laughter, follow after."

Thanks Mom, I Love You.

Who is to say, that she may have been right when she said, most all of us really fall in Love only once. Any others before and after are not real Love. My mother was a very caring, accomplished, real and a down to earth yet independent human being. I hope some of her traits show in me. Strangely enough, my father had all the same traits, but he did not give me anything to write in my book.

I Love You Dad.

5

If you've made it to this page
you've probably already said,
That's not true or maybe you've
said there are many different kinds
of Love and all of them can't be considered
the next best thing to insanity.
IF SO, I agree...
There is no doubt
that <u>unconditional Love</u> is true Love.
It can't be controlled
or interfered with
and is nowhere near insanity.
However, even if you agree with
the title, keep in mind that the words
"I LOVE YOU" shouldn't be taken
or used lightly. Although they are
only words, someone's actions will speak much
louder than any words will ever come
close to saying
and
Even when you think you're in Love,
you may act a little, or a great deal
like you're crazy.
That's why I believe that...
Love is the next best thing to Insanity.

Randon

Are you doing the same things
over and over...
and expecting different results?

Falling in Love,
Being in Love
and Staying in Love

are three entirely different things.

The TRUTH...
the WHOLE TRUTH and
Nothing But the TRUTH
are three entirely different things...
and that's the TRUTH,
THE WHOLE TRUTH and
Nothing But THE TRUTH...
So help me, ME...
who else?

_____

While we're at it... just remember that
'NO ONE', not even Me could LOVE YOU as much
as I do.

After all that I've been through...

in Love, for years and years and time after time, I'm still optimistic about Love and relationships, the things people say that they mean when they say them, the promises that they make to one another in hoping the happiness that they share lasts forever and never ends; I can safely say that I am a soldier of LOVE.

That was really a long sentence...you didn't believe all that did you?

In the beginning...
eyes meet and
the seed is planted and growing
and
THE THUNDER AND LIGHTENING
are just
coming into view...

Pray for the flower to grow,
for you will never know
the storm that lay in store
for you
when someone says...
I Love you!

When we first started dating,
do you remember how much
I missed you
and you missed me,
when I was gone?

Well, why don't I miss you anymore?

Cause you never leave!

For those of you,

who have a mutual, meaningful, Loving, happy, fun-filled, joyful, wonderful, physical, trusting, creative, and fulfilled relationship that seems so natural and harmonious and everlasting;

Don't worry that all will change

but

seriously,

if you seem to fall into that
description above,

please cherish what you have. Appreciate and
acknowledge each other,
for you each truly
have possession of the most important and rewarding
commodity on this planet.

But have you ever wondered,
are you

YOUR OWN WORST ENEMY?

HOT DANG, DIPITEE-DOOO.

Now that's a question you can ponder on your little old cranium for a few miniscule minutes out of your grueling, fairytale, one-sided, self-centered, perfect pictured life.

So eventually... some
we forgive and forget.

Some
we forgive
but don't
forget.

Some we don't forgive
and never forget.

So why don't you just
forget me
and
I'll forgive you.

Thank you,

Randon '84

14

For most of us...

what's really important in life doesn't
really seem important in our younger years,
our inexperienced years.

BUT...

When we're older, what was so terribly
important when we were younger, isn't
important anymore.

So why do so many of us wish to be younger
again when we get older?

Is it really so important to be older and
wiser?

If you are older, think of all the things you
didn't know --- when you were younger
and
if you're a young
whippersnapper,
try and think of all
the things you're going to learn.

Sorry,

it doesn't work that way...
and if you're young, this all
may not be important
because
you've got more important
things to do
than to try and figure out
what's really important in
life, RIGHT?

I can remember

one particular relationship... when the hardest thing
for me to understand was trying to understand
someone who didn't understand anything.

Did you understand any of that?

Two things this book can't do...
make decisions for you
or
teach you
HOW TO MAKE LOVE...

LAST,

ha, fooled ya'.

Sorry!

No matter what anyone says...

you have to learn

The hard way...

SIMPLE!

and
Things all seem to be
really stupid
when you're trying
to deal with someone...

who's too stupid to know
how STUPID
they are...
Damn it!

When 'two' people are in Love, it's
the most incredible feeling that anyone could ever
try to imagine.

S I M P L Y,

Love is great!

Sometimes

Because I Love you

I'll give you my heart
but remember,

it still belongs to me.

It's so sad that so few people appreciate

something when it's given to them.

It's much better if they have to work

for it.

So I wonder what condition this gift will

be in, when you decide you

don't want it anymore?

'The Author'

INFINITY'S CRUSADER

I've been everywhere,
sometimes cheated, sometimes treated fair.
I've flown soaring high
with the clouds in my eyes,
and
spied on Kings and Queens that no one could spy.

Drifted aloft and all alone
with God as my only overtone.

'Twas I once with a band of
little rainbow smugglers
and once again with Cinderella
and her three sissty ugglers.

I've tamed the worst of hurricanes
and spawned
the fiercest cyclones that could never be tamed.

Had all the answers when no questions were asked
and always been first when there was no last.

Played the game when there was no game to play...
and said it all when there was nothing to say.

I've' Loved for Love and I've Loved for money
and
laughed so much 'til it wasn't even funny.

I've forgotten today and had the morrow
to remember the sorrow
of being...
all these things, that must come to pass and follow.

Created creation and had nothing to see...
and
been all that could be with nothing for me.

I've stared death cold in the face
and scowled from its grasp with astonishing grace.

Manned the plank of Captain Hook
but never a thing I stole or took.

Enchanted the heart of The Most Beautiful Woman
but found her beauty a most deadly omen.

I've traveled through time... 'til the end of forever,
to trick and to fool the cleverest of cleaver.
and
I've searched the world over to find
and totally revealed to my mind,
that The Wisest Man of All,
to whom fate shall never call
is the man who knows all...
and says nothing.

Sound familiar?

I'll Love you... until
the end
of forever...
and
never, no never
shall this bond
of Love... ever
be severed...
How clever.

___

Never... may be forever
but
Forever... may be...
Never!

I hope you remember this forever
and never... forget.

I remember a conversation with my oldest son one day
over a Chinese lunch.
He was sixteen and had discovered something
for himself called women, well... girls, and he was
telling me how his girlfriend had come to him and said
she was going back to her old boyfriend.
My son said he told her to 'go get screwed.'
I simply replied..."She probably did."

Later he started in again,
"Dad, does this mean
I'm gonna' feel bad
for a long time now?"
I replied, "Son...when we end a relationship,
we usually feel really bad
for about half as long as the
amount of time we
were involved!"
He replied very seriously,
"Oh, Gee Dad...
does this mean I'll feel
this bad
for three whole days?"

Real Illusion

It's the middle of the night.
Thoughts of you...
in this absence of light...
create a smile
just for a while.
My present mood is changing
soon to be gone.
My moody blues are leaving
with this vision of you...
turning me on.
I see your hair, so long,
caressing one side
of the flowing lines
of your sensuous and sexual shoulders.
They revive my glances
to your beckoning eyes.
As you call my name
while seducing my mind
to find your lips,
so sexually sublime
and gently persuade
these moistened treasures
you've so givingly
named mine.

"Please kiss me" you say
Give me all - you've got
and
Into my lips you'll stay...
and I'll give back the lust this Love has been taught.
For a moment...
it all seems so real
and then the black of this night
seems to steal...
your lips away,
until once more I can recreate
this illusion
that once was really real.

We all...

eventually

live...

the realities

of our own

ILLUSIONS!

A gift from God and Me

Here's just one of God's little flowers,
to remind you of the hours,
spent us two together,
in memories that will forever,
stay locked in Lover's glow,
and never letting go...
as only you should know,
and as this flower grows,
giving all the Love it shows,
hold you close to me...
yesterday, Now and Never!
For when this rose has wilted and died,
you'll know, how hard I tried,
to give my Love, to the one who lied,
to me, to herself and her pride.

Love,
~~Brandon~~

I'm checking into the hospital
Monday,
I'm scheduled for brain surgery
Tuesday
to have you surgically removed
from my mind.
But my doctor says
There's a 50/50 chance there'll be a
big scar.

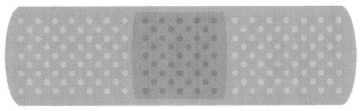

For brain # 1

and

brain # 2

Note: This one for brain #2 only applies to us guys.

Remember when...

we first met and you promised to always... be totally
honest with me?

That was your first lie!

What justifies a lie?

Think about it.
If we were all liars...
what value would be
placed on TRUTH?

How would anyone know
when someone was telling
the TRUTH?

If TRUTH could be determined,
most, if not all the liars
couldn't handle it.
So how do you feel about someone
you've told the TRUTH to
and they don't believe you, or the TRUTH?
Be truthful.

This next one is for you
and if it's all I ever do
I'll simply say that

I hope someone really Loves you.

So o o o o o o o o o o o o o o o o...

If you want a really heavy relationship...
just pretend you're a lead brick
in Love with a
TWO-TON TRUCK.

I'm in Lust

Hi!

I think I Love___ yoooouu.

This is incredible.

Wow! You really turn me on.

Light switch!

You're really neat!

Ding! Dong!

What's that?

I don't know, but it feels good.

Do it again.

PLEASE...

what's your name?

What?

Wow!

Really! Oh, gosh!

Gee!

Look at those eyes.

Did you see that? Did you feeeeeel THAAAAT?

Somebody stop me!

Take it easy!
Slow down!
Everything will be there tomorrow!
Don't go so fast!

Anytime is a good time
but
right now is best!
but

If you don't, then you won't.

If you won't, then you can't.

so

go for it

Now!

Try to remember...

that a Love affair is no different
from anything else in life,
that turns out to be worthwhile.
because
If you're willing to take the chance,

then you have to be willing to take the
loss.

As a glimmering reflection
from the past
shall twinkle in a Lover's eye...

True Love is to know
real Love will last
and that it will never die.

Never may be forever
BUT
Forever may be
Never!

This just keeps poppin' up

The Greatest Problem

The simplicities of life on this planet
are greatly
overlooked
yet undoubtedly are
the most
Important!

Randon 1986

Definitions

Randon - Forceful
OOOOOOOOOH, Really?

Thorn - Anything or anyone that occasions discomfort, pain or annoyance.

Aaaaaaaaaw!

Vicious Cycle

Once I had a dream that I was insane. 'No offense to any of you Lovers out there or anyone else that has mental problems.'
ANYWAY...
I was trapped in a nut house and I don't mean a place where walnuts and almonds are grown. After months of study, my doctors determined that what I needed was someone to Love me and I would be cured!
Remember this is a dream...
One day, while on a therapy trip to the park, I met someone. We fell in Love and she saved me from the nut house. Yeah!

We were together for nearly three years, until she finally drove me crazy.

So now she just sends me cookies... in care of the nut house.

Sometimes...
words unspoken... are an apology
well rehearsed by a truly tearful heart.

When I sit alone in the dark...

It seems the more I think about the
reasons for us not being together anymore,
the more unreasonable the reasons
become...

but
just because
there aren't any guarantees in Life,
doesn't mean
that you've got to be too afraid
to feel...
and do...
what you want to.

I only Love you
and that's all I really want to do.

No rings,
No strings,

No imaginary things...
just all the Love and joy
that this relationship brings.

My heart has a question

Only the heart has the vision... to see clearly.
What is essential is invisible to the eye.

Cause and effect can make a Lover very leery,
by changing a Love affair into a lonely lie.

And why are the reasons for parting Lovers
so many and absurd?

It's a question without an answer
with an answer in every word.

And not time, deceit, nor infidelity
will ever obscure
the fate that a poor Lover's heart
must endure.

The thought of you being with me is
almost as nice as you...

being with me,
but...
not quite.

I Love you!
I miss you!

Now just where the hell are you?

An attempted dramatic and romantic
theatrical
Love affair...

you were...
'Wonder Woman'
and
I was 'Superman'...

Neither one of us
got the Part.

Oop-poop-pee-OOPS!

Lust making Love

Sensitive touch...
is this a vision of my Love?

I'm lame...
I'll surely go insane...
unless I learn how to control
this feeling I feel for her
and knowing she feels the same.

We're not playing games.
Just say either of our names,
in a crowd
softly or loud...
and we both feel cold chills
and remember the thrills...
of when we make Love.
Is it Lust?...
Surely not!

It has to be Love and will last...

And then somehow
just for now...
it's all in the past.

Love making,
Love taking...

Or
is a memory forever...
the price we must pay...
when we can say,

I once felt the Lust of Love's
most cherished endeavor.

Randon

I think
I'll start writing
fortune cookies...
because I believe that

all that is regretted
or
is of bad being
is
Usually brought upon ourselves
by ourselves.

One Kiss
is worth
a thousand
words

So please, just...
KISS OFF! Uh!

I mean... SO PLEASE KISS!

K- eep
I- t
S- imple
S- tupid

The way something is said

or the conditions of which are present,
completely affect the feeling that
someone might have about a situation.

But the result of the statement
or the feeling left
is entirely up to the person listening.

And what someone thinks

doesn't necessarily
make it that certain way
or make it a truth.

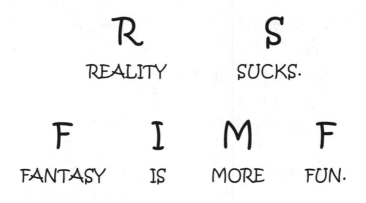

R   S

REALITY   SUCKS.

F   I   M   F

FANTASY   IS   MORE   FUN.

Uh-huh, when you first saw this, you thought
it was something DIRTY... didn't you?

What you See...

is what you get

isn't it?

Bull Poo Poo!

Sometimes using a little
psychology in a Love affair
straightens out a lot of the
problems.

But the only thing
that I dislike...
about psychology,
is all of its
'Psychological'
game playing
Bull Shit!

Scuuuuuse me!
BUT
nothing else sounded quite right.

Actually I think it's OK to play games in a relationship...
just as long as you play them with my rules.

The Greatest Lie

The **last thing,** I would ever
want you to do...
is fall in Love
with me.

Have you ever heard
someone say
"I'll never fall in Love again?"
It almost sounds like a song.
Don't you
think
they meant
to say...
'I never want to be hurt
in Love again?'

When I'm alone

When I stop what I'm doing
no matter where I am
to think about you,
it's usually when I'm alone.

I can remember mostly the good
and every now and then...
some of the bad.

It seems the longer it's been since
I've touched you, seen you or
made Love to you,
the more unrealistic, what we had
seems to be.
It becomes the most realistic feeling
while you're not with me and feeling
that you are... while
I try to accept the
feeling that I realize, you will never touch me,
see me, make Love to me, or hear my
voice again for as long as I live.
I start to dwell on the unfairness of
IT ALL...
and then it always ends with the same thought...
that maybe somehow, somewhere,
you're thinking
the same thing...

Don't be
overly cautious...
with someone
who's
more cautious
than you are.

WELL THAT'S SMART!

IIIIIIIII don't know...
I probably wouldn't do that if I were you.

What turns on a boy-beer?

What else?

BEER-BUST!

I'm lonely again

I'm pulling up the covers more
but I'm still cold.
Another flash, I see your face again!
Now I'm staring at the dark.

I reach to place my arm under your breast
and pull you next to me
laying your head on my shoulder.

I listen to the dark
and want your soft sweet voice
beside me once more
as the words "I Love you" flow
across my pillow
and linger in my ear just for a moment
before you reassure my insecurity
with your soft kiss.

The following is Rated PG -
'Pretty Good'

As we make Love,
I hear your voice over and over again,
"I Love you Baby,"
"I Love you so much,"

"I Love you Baby"...

The echo goes on and on
and on...

and then once more I'm pulling up the covers
but I'm still cold
and I realize you're really gone
and I'm alone again.

Mind over matter

Pardon the pun, but the individual who
uses mind over matter is indeed very intelligent.
DUH!
Since 1981 A.Y. (After You)
I have conditioned my mind
to the fact that maybe you...
Don't Matter,
as it was in 1980 B.Y. (Before You)

Why am I still talkin' about that?
I guess it took me that long
to believe what I just said.

There is definitely
one thing in this
Civilized? world,
that
I can absolutely be totally
sure of...
that society will <u>eventually</u> change
me into everything that I've tried
so hard
not
to be...
for
so... long!
Maybe

While living...
my life —
I've developed a strength
that's very hard
to come by.
Yet,
I'm leaving my sensitivity
behind!

and

I know that I really deserve
anything that
I will achieve in life,
because I've certainly
labored long and hard
for what I don't have.

By the way...
happiness is being happy with what you have...
Whatever that may be.
AND
I know I'm right, when I say...

NO ONE can make us happy.

We have to be happy first...
with who we are
and
what we have or think we have.
And if we're LUCKY, we may find...
someone that might make us happier.

I know I'm right about this... because

I'm never wrong.

I thought I was wrong once,

but I was...
Wrong!

The Reality of Time

A wondrous mysterious thing so small
that feels no pain,
taking all and giving nothing
taking nothing and giving all the same.
Ageing and wrinkling the beauty,
giving life as if it were a duty.
Taking all the Love and hate,
giving the prolonging wait.
Stopping the worry and fear,
making a point to hurry there and here.
Synchronizing the clock of fate
and distorting all that participates.
Making a Love affair today,
tomorrow taking it away.
Changing day into night
while it holds on so very tight.
Looking for it everywhere,
finding it nowhere.
Why doesn't it care?
Time can cure, time can kill,
I am sure, that IS its' will...
It won't stand still.

Its' mountains will grow,
its' seas will cease to be
but
one thing it will never do,
is lie to you or me.

My life is in its' hands
and
I am only what I am...
Nothing less, nothing more,
Until time closes that final door.
It takes away all that I do
but
can never take
the memory of you.

Out of sight,

out of mind?

Bull Poo Poo!

Open your eyes — look carefully...

What you see...
standing in front of you...
might not be
what you think it is.

A very profound statement...

The truth...
is always beautiful!
Which is a lie!

Look into my eyes...

Don't be afraid of me.

I Love you.

You're probably more afraid of yourself
than me.
I would never hurt you... will not desert you...

I Love you.

If you won't believe your eyes,
then look into mine.

Theresa Pain

Oh my Theresa...
who at first I did not want.
Oh how I miss her
while mind and heart she taunts.

As the dreams of her all Loving me
the nights seem to steal...
and oh how she Loved me
and so she told me was real.

And oh how I believed her
not knowing the pain,
though warned by one,
that lay waiting for me,

once I set her free.
To never as long as I live
ever again
touch or hear her or see,
a Lover who will never come again
with as passionate a Love as had we.

Oh my darling, my little 10
who once called me sweetheart
but nearly drove me insane.
I once Loved you
and
I forgive you
my Theresa Pain.

Randon 1981

I'll make a deal with you
that you can't refuse.

Just let me be what and who I am...
and I'll do the same for you.
signed,
your Loving Lover agent
for life!
Ha! Ha!

Flutter-byes are Free

Let me be free
let me do
what I want to be
but Love me
and I will Love you.
In the beginning
I will hold you
as long as I must,
whether it be for Love or lust
or more nurtured trust.
When we touch, if only for a second,
'Total Love' will be reckoned.
I will Love until you no longer care.
Just let me know when Love is no longer there
and I'll be gone like the wind
to find Love's better friend…
and what we had will remember the new,
of when our eyes first met
and of when there was only you.
I'll search for Love again and again,
while feeling your heart as my heart's twin,
and knowing
that my going
'Shall never be our End'
because

I Love you…   Randon

I used to think that age
didn't make any difference
but now I know I'm right.

The only things that AGE me are
the DIFFERENCES.

In all of our differences
and power struggles...
along with the uneasy goodbyes and tears
and anything else that goes with
feeling sorry for ourselves and why has this someone
done this to me.
How many of us realize
that they did it to us because
we let them?

Isn't it true that opposites attract
and that we always want
what we think we can't have?

I'm certainly overjoyed that I found out
what you were all about...
Before you did.

I'm convinced

There doesn't have to be a reason
for everything
and
I'm not going to worry about it.

Now why did I just say all that?

There's got to be a reason!

Although amazing, but true...
most of us jump out of one set of
problems...
that we convince ourselves we can't take
anymore...

just to jump right back into a different set
of problems...
which may be **worse** than the old set...
realizing way too late, we'd have been
better off where we were in the other
relationship
we just totally ruined.

Me, Me, Me, Me, Me, Me,
I, I, I, I, I !

In every relationship I've ever had,
I learned
a great deal. However, the greatest thing I
learned in the one I just had with you, was
that I STILL HAVE a great deal to learn.

What you think
someone feels
about you,
in as much as you think...
that they Love you,
or that you Love them,
is only an illusion
created by your mind
to satisfy the need
that you have...

to 'be not alone'.

Now, come on...
think about it and give it a

CHANCE!

Until I had lived through and gotten over...

and remembered my first two or three
Loves,

I thought 'Melancholy' was a dog that

picked watermelons.

THE DISTANCE

When you took your trip and had to
leave me behind,
I thought I would die
but
the farther you got from me
and the longer you stayed away... it seemed
the closer we became,
until you never came back.
Oops...
but
You know, No matter what you said or did
or what I said or did,
you can never stop me from Loving you.
You're not here with me now
but you are somehow.
There was never...
any doubt, in my mind that I Loved you.
In fact, I still do Love you
and I imagine that I always will...
and I forgive you...
but
I will never _____
forget!

I have the strength
to accept that
I Love you...

Do you have the strength...
to accept

That I do?

Nobody's perfect...

and SO...
I'll admit I'm guilty of Loving you,
So what's my sentence...
LIFE?

or

I guess I could plead 'Not Guilty'
by reason of Insanity.

And then I'd be Free, and have a life...
of my own...
alone.

For you to leave me
would be very cruel
But...
Not as cruel as if
I lost the power to remember us
Or...
if we never were.

When I finally realized
that I had to deal with you
not being around anymore _____
It was very hard to deal with.

Cheese!
Why can't we just get
past...
The Past?

There are times I sit alone in the dark
and want you with me again.

I imagine me holding you...

But

The more I begin to realize why I miss you
the more I wonder... if I really want you back.

And Now,

    that I've really had some time
        to think about it, a LOT...

    I think you need to give me a break AND try
    giving yourself a chance to forgive ME...
      For ALL the bad things...

I 'Never' did to you.

On occasion, I ask myself ---
Even though I wrote this book,
have I really ever read it?

WELLLLLLLLLLLL, MAYBE!

"Though lonely, I can dream"

I am the unknown creator.
Though I alone
have known
The common denominator.

I am the architect of Love,
the dweller of Life,
the surveyor of
the eternal strife,

for man and beast
to have their feast
and the 'God of the Wind' on high
that will finally fly...
into the heart of you my dear
and quickly blow away the fear
of having me so near...
For I am the one who Loves you

and I have tasted all your tears.

Randon

I want to be strong and soft,
willing and knowing,
free and flowing,
gentle as the lamb,
wise as the serpent.

But I am only what I am.
Forgive me for being so selfish,
and trying to be

just
a man.

Tell it like it is

Do you know why
I never lie to you?

Because you trust me.

So why do you think
I lie to you
when I do?

Because that's when
you don't trust me.

Honesty is...
NOT
always the best policy.

and

that's a lie...

which is the truth.

During circumcision,

where does the doctor
put the excess?

The peter pan,

where else!

What happens when
little boy
Smurf
meets little girl
Smurf
and he falls in Love
with her?

SMURF'S
UP!

The following page
points out
The six C's
for having
a completely successful
Love Affair...

Compassion,

Consideration,

Commitment,

Communication,

Courage

and

Cash

And now...
for the $64,000 question.

Do I really Love, or
Do I Love, that someone Loves me?

or

does that someone just <u>tell me</u> they

Love ME?

Tricky!

Believe me

How do I know that I Love you?
Because I have the eyes,
the heart and hands
to see and feel you.

How do you know that you Love me?
Because you believe what you see,

touch and feel...
and we and Love are real

and I Love you

Believe me.

Touching a memory of you

What's in a touch
that you've missed so much...
when warm nights were so new
while I was holding you?

Remember that bliss
when you felt my kiss?
so badly now I miss.

The memory strong, so very strong
for our Love so deep, I truly long.

and

Now that I am alone...
my heart has seen
what my mind has sewn.

As one weathers through
the Love relationship affairs of their lives,
they begin to realize that after a while
the ending of each one becomes
a little easier...
WELL,... Maybe
and
When you look back at an affair
that you just passed through
and say "that's life!"
Then you've definitely got it down 'pat'
so to speak.
And remember ... by the time you're
250
ending a Love relationship affair will be as easy
as a piece of cake.

Seriously,
A Love affair...
is only what you make it.

NOW
that was brilliant!

I'll be signing autographs over that one.

OH YEH', SAME TO YOU!
but seriously,
I'm just kidding
I'm serious!

Should I ask your forgiveness
For Loving you?

Or just simply thank you
For letting me?
OR
Should you ask my forgiveness
For Loving me?

Or just simply thank me
For letting you?

Your
Imagination
IS YOUR ONLY
Limitation

Why is it,
every time
that the last thing
we need _____
is the first thing we do...
Like fall in Love?

Good question!

Twenty-One Words

Heavy breath,
fuzzy vision,
heart beating fast.

Scold the stress!
If I make the incision,

I'll be...
in Love at last.

Whew!

What's the #1 cause of divorce?
What else?

Marriage!

_____

What's a legal marriage?

Two people in Love...
with a marriage license.

SO...

What's an 'ill-eagle' marriage?

Two BIG sick birds...
in Love

but they can't get a license.

Multiple Choice

a) Together,

b) Apart,

c) Fighting...

Which word makes you feel better?

Duuuuuuuuuuh!

Just one Love like you
is all I'll ever need...

NEXT!

Broken hearts
usually mend
very strongly
And
usually have no weaknesses...

So if you want a really strong heart...

just go out and find someone
to break your heart a few times.

And...

then your heart will be really strong.

The genuine human

heart...

knows not a stranger.
But once that heart has been broken
it wishes it had never known.

In Love, we are all different...
But really, we're all alike.

and just remember...

Love is a stranger that we all
eventually...
get to know
but
can never trust.

Maybe...

A letter to myself and you

Is a loss the birth of an oncoming gain?
Whatever it is
When you have it,
Let yourself feel the pain.
Don't hold back your hurt.
Let it flow for a while.
Give it a chance to have its' trial.

What you've Loved that you've lost,
is eventually worth it at all cost.
Experience is the best teacher
and every heart learns how
to make it a little easier.

You must accept you're a very small speck
in this vast order of time
but that you can go on alone
and keep some rhythm and rhyme.

To have lost something you've Loved or wanted,
is better than never to have been flaunted.
And after a while
you'll find...
a change in your style.

Try a little of yourself out on the town.
Try to make a smile out of a frown, upside down.
Soon you'll see that you're much stronger now...
just for today you can't see how.

But tomorrow is truth
just wait and see.

You can remember when you said "I Love you"
and "I forgive you"
But remember,
You also should have said,
"I Love me."

Speaking of letters...

What do you call
A 'man' who carries the mail?

A mailman... of course.

So what do you call
a woman who carries the mail?

A femail man.
What else?

Tonight's menu for Lovers...
Steak... REALLY?
parsley – Yuck!
biscuits and butter,
broccoli and cheese,
wine and YOU (obviously the best part).

Sometimes
I think I'll have you for dessert
But...
what kind of topping will I use?
Maybe I'll just have you plain.

A Fantasy

Try to imagine a streak of light
on a evening flight
to somewhere in space
to find the face
of the one who loves me.

How quickly it moves
as it quests to soothe
my need for you
forever and to
be mine alone,
'til the air turns to stone
and straw into gold will be sewn.

So imagine these things to be,
as real as you,
as real as me,
and forever we will be,
what we want to be,
just free
and
a fantasy...

Everything must change!

I knew it was time for a change in the
relationship when I realized that
I had her...
right where <u>she wanted me!</u>

If ONLY...
I would listen to me!

Sad, but true...

Traveling through life, after a time
you may find
Sometimes having
is not so pleasant a thing
as wanting.

Don't ever deny that you're in denial...
just admit it...

Oh now what?...You can't admit that you're in denial...
Well just forget it then.
Oh... don't tell me that you can't forget it.

Then just STOP... What now, you can't STOP?
What is this?
What do you mean, WHAAAAAAAAT is
WHAT?

Well then... is ending this 'never ending',
'I'm in Love relationship',
seeming just a little crazy or insane?

Today's Lesson in Spelling
for LOVERS
Only!
Be honest with yourself...
Can you do that?
OK
Spell the word Lover.
L-O-V-E-R
Good!
Now, take the "L" out and what
do you have?

Did you laugh when you
realized what it
spells?
There'ssssssssssssssssssssssssssssssss...
a great deal more to a relationship than just being
someone's LOVER.
Lover is made up of two words... LOVE and OVER.
But it's fun while it lasts.

Once Upon a Time

Once I thought, you thought
that I was everything you ever
wanted,
and then...
I found out that you didn't know
what it was that you wanted.

and

DID we live happily ever after?
Not!

Twenty-Twenty

I once thought that losing your Love
was as cruel and as harsh and unfair
as losing my sight.

But since our separation...
I have much better vision.

After many, many enlightening
episodes in my life,

I've learned to ask
basically nothing of anyone...

and therefore, I continue getting
nothing from anyone!

I'm so committed to 'our' relationship that before long,

someone
may have me committed!

You control your Destiny!

Learning what 'NOT' to do... can be priceless.

Lately,

I've been so worried
about you

and what
you've
been
doing,

that
I've forgotten
about me.

Well

Hello

Me,

Where the Hell have
you
Been?

I don't think...

I'll ever forget
that last day that I saw you.
I'll always remember you
were the one
who wanted to leave.
You were the one
who let the stranger in.
I regretted and still
regret
seeing you go...
Although
I wasn't the one
who asked you to leave,
I don't think I'll ever be the one
to ask you to come back!
Actually I feel as though I
don't really care if you come
back to me or not... or do I?
and I'll miss you...
and I do Love you...
and I think I have to go now...I think I'm gonna' Cry!

All you really Red Hot Lovers...
Can really identify with the next page...

A Love affair we both can share

I need some catsup
please hurry up!
Why won't it come out?
Hold it up, shake it up
scream and shout!

If this were any worse
surely I'd be cursed
with eating my food
in a little better mood.

My plate just can't wait.
I need some catsup now, and how!
Please hurry up,
Oh, look, WOW!

It's coming out now,
It's coming out now,
It's gushing out now,

HELP!....Help!....
THAT'S ENOUGH STOP!
OH, GOD GET THE MOP!

There's catsup falling on the floor.
It's running down my leg
and right out the door.
My sandwich bread is all gushy and red.
I should have stayed in bed!

It's oozing outside,
just like the red tide.
There's catsup everywhere
people are starting to stare.

The goop has overcome. AAAHHHHH!

BUT, AT LEAST
I FINALLY GOT SOME!

Where does a salad go to pick up another salad and have a few drinks?

You guessed it —
a salad bar.

Are YOU happy,
with who YOU are?

Do YOU like YOU?

If YOU don't and aren't
then
YOU need to do something about
IT! 'you'

Don't let YOU get in the way of your happiness...

WHO ARE YOU ANYWAY?

Take my advice please!

If you Love something, it's true-
Set it free and it will come back to you.

If you want it to be your own,
develop an open-minded tone.
And when it returns
treat it well, don't stall.
Be gracious and kind,
a little less heart
and a little more mind.

Hold on gently please!
Or you'll lose it all.
Don't accuse, don't abuse
for you and yourself
are the ones who will loose.

I totally believe

that

Finding Love

works the same way
catching butterflies does...
in that,
just like the Butterfly Catcher,
who Loves to catch butterflies with a big net,
can't understand why it's so hard to catch the
butterflies.
And
Can't understand why those butterflies
are always trying to get away...
especially after they've been caught.

If the Butterfly Catcher would just be still
and patient and just sit down
in the middle of the field...

After a while,

the
Butterflies of Love
will just
land on their shoulder.

Is anybody listening?

What?

You really need to listen a little
to most of the next
few lines.

Sometimes...
the things you think you really need the most,
may be something you may need a little...

but

not the most of what you really need.

So make the most of something
no matter how little of it
you get or need.

I used to think that Loving you was
terribly difficult at times but...
I find missing you
is a real <u>BITCH</u>!

A thought too devastating to ponder...
that I might be so simple as a rose.

For I would too quickly wilt and die
and you would never hold me close again...

but not for the fear of my thorns.

Never Say Never

for
had I known my heart
would break so easily,
I would never have unwrapped it
and left it out in the open.

_____

I would never say...
Never say NEVER!

Thanks Hart.

Imagine

It's raining outside
but we still have
some champagne...
The rain
was made
for champagne...
I wonder how it would
taste...
If I just poured it all
over you
and made a toast to
Love?

Practice makes Perfect...
and
Rejection... is supposed to build
Character
and
I've had a lot of
Practice.

Maybe I knew you once

Don't I know you from somewhere,
I recognize that stare,
that look in your eyes,
I know I know you from somewhere.
Didn't we use to Love each other
or something like that?
Now I remember...
You're the one that told me...
you Loved me so much,
that you were in Love with me.

But that was a long time ago.
Don't you remember...
well, maybe not...
I guess I've made a mistake...
Goodbye!

AREEVIDURCHEE
BABY!

I really Love my memories about past Loves...
but I use to have a very bad memory though...

if I remember correctly.

Then one day I FORGOT that I had a bad memory,
and now I can remember everything.

So if I forgot that I had a bad memory,
how did I know that I had a bad memory?

I can't remember.

BUT

I do remember my first girlfriend...
who introduced me to Love making.

On our first perfect evening...
we decided to go for it
And...

we headed for the bedroom...

About 10 feet from the bedroom door I stopped
and said, "Wait a minute... I have to warn you."
She said, "Oh no...what?"

I quickly replied, "This may take 7 or 8 hours."
As she leaned back and then started to laugh,
she leaned over and kissed me very softly,
and with a very serious look on her face...
said "Oh!!!
Why so quick?"

If you once Loved something very Strongly
and Deeply...
and you let it slip right through your
fingers...

Then you were definitely using
Too much
SOAP IN THE SHOWER.

Being Miserable is
ONLY

a state of mind...

Fortunately,
same thing goes for HAPPY.

Which one do you want to be?
The key word here is want.
Well...do you want to be happy?

Then be happy and shut up!
STOP with all the BS.
If you're reading this...you're alive,
aren't you?

Be careful
If you're a guy...

And you're really trying
to feel what a woman's heart...
really feels like.

You may find yourself
right in the middle of
a booby trap.

I used to think of a lot of things
that were really great, like...
caramel crunch ice cream,
Kailua and coffee,
hang-gliding and skin diving...
then I met you!
WOW!

Some things to think about...

Please put on your thinking cap,
this may get deep.

Just about everything that happens to all
of us, in our relationships,
GOOD or BAD, revolves around our
Self Image.
The type of relationship that we may attract or begin
is determined by our Self Image.
and
No matter what you say, think or feel,
admit or do...
You live for acknowledgement!

Although
Love may be the answer...

Why is Perception everything?

I believe I recall hearing someone say
that there is no reality... there is only
perception.
That's why so many people think being
intimate with someone is having sex with
them.

SORRY...Intimacy and having SEX
are no where near... the same thing.

And while we're at it,
I know for a fact that
Character is never developed...

it's ONLY revealed
in a time of
need.

To have you is too revealing,
to hold you is to limit your spirit...
to caress you is an obsession so willing
that my heart wishes to possess
and hope you not fear it.
But possess you I can not,
for you would not be free...
and free you must be
so as to Love me.

ALWAYS being RIGHT
is exactly
the WRONG thing to be...

Right?

A really sad but true decision...

I'd rather leave you
and have you wanting me back,
than to stay
and have you wanting me to leave
and
Never come back.

When you go...
All I know...
Of life, Of Love and laughter,
Follow After!

One evening...
My mom and I were talking about
a girlfriend I had broken up with.
I said, "but mom,
you don't understand,
she is so beautiful."
My mom asked,
"Is she beautiful on the inside or the outside?"
I said, "the outside,
her face, eyes, hair,
skin, legs, fingernails,
her whole body is just
beautiful."
My mom replied,

"None of Those Things
will last very long!"

Sometimes...

Lovers
are rather like
hemorrhoids.
They can get to be a real pain in the
butt...
And once you get rid of them
you pray they'll
never come back.

If you made it this far, you may be saying…
There certainly are a lot of negative things
in this book. But if you really think about
most of them, you might admit that they're
true.
If you've been through a relationship or a
few…
then you should know, most of the things you've
read are true.

And by the way,

Always tell the truth…
Especially when you don't want anyone to believe you.

Your delusional expectations
in a relationship...
will create
your own dilemma...

unless you expect nothing.

But then you may end up with

Nothing...

Unless you find someone
who Really cares about you...
and expects
Nothing!

The one most incredibly honest thing an
x-girlfriend ever said to me was,

"I'm not really completely honest with you."

and then...

While rolling my eyes, I replied "So, do you
expect me to believe that?"

Ego, can create perception...
but
Wisdom desolves deception.

One person in Love...
'SINGLE'

Two people in Love...
'DYNAMIC DUO'

Three people in Love...
'THREESOME THAT SCREAMS SOME'

Four people in Love...
'FOURMIDABLE'

Five people in Love...
ORGY? OOPS!

Sorry,

Sounds like The Jerry Springer Show.

Some simply simple rules...

I
DEMAND
that you stop placing so many
DEMANDS
on our relationship!
and if
you don't
STOP
giving me ultimatums,
I'll have to give you an ultimatum
and
don't be jealous,
it
just shows
how insecure
YOU really are!

Hang in there!

It's almost over...
Famous last words.

It ain't over 'til it's over.

How can I put it into words?

Breaking up...
Am I lost again?
Am I happy again?
My mind is traveling.
Just for now I'll try
to forget the past, the
hurt I feel.
Save it for a rainy day
and have it with a little
crying on the rocks or
maybe straight.
Who will let me feel and
have enough perception to
understand why you're not
my Lover anymore.
Who am I talking to?
Who is asking all the
questions?
Do I know you?
Do you have any answers?
Where am I?

Randon

Anything you achieve in life
is manifested by three words,
"I have decided."

Then the fun part
is doing it.

For those who have Loved

For when there was Love
for all the good years,
for all the tears,
I honor you.
I understand you.
I can share your whole life with you.
I know that someone new
is waiting for you
and tomorrow you'll see
it's much better to be
one of those who have Loved
like me.

Take my advice again... please.
  Although Love letters can be wonderful...

If you receive a Love letter from someone who
"professes"
their undying, never ending, everlasting Love... and
they swear they will never stop Loving you and they
will Love you forever...
Go on and read the front of the letter...
Of course,
and then turn it over to the back where nothing is
written...
and try to read what it doesn't say.

Masters of Love

We are the Masters.
We are the strong.
Looking and seeking
to find the not weeping.
Only to see that we
ARE ALONE.

You don't always
get
what you think
you want...

"There is a God!"

I'll remember
you
every day of my life...

Will you do the
same for me?

Do you think you're
really in Love
with someone?

How do you know?

What makes you believe
that you are?

Oh really?
well then...

Prove it!

I remember
ONE particular
evening... just one?
If I remember correctly,
you started with
all the, "you never this"
and "you never that"...
I responded with,
"Well... I can't remember
you **ever agreeing**
with
a single thing I've ever said."

You replied, "**I disagree!**"

Are you powerful enough
to over power
someone's
Power Trip?

Be gentle,
be smart,
be honest,
be gone,
be happy,
be independent,
Be Free!

True Love...

Gives you the right
to be free.
Do you think you Love
someone?

Do you Love them for who they are...
Or
what you want them
to Be?

Secretly Yours

Again,
The night is still...
Visions...
of your face,
that my heart embraces...
come and go
at will.

And now, your lips press mine
and your eyes such a treasure
to find,
caress my body...
and yours and mine
so heavenly entwined
in a making of Love,
that will never be forgotten
by time.

I pause for an instant
to dwell on the feeling,
that I'm feeling
so real.

Then suddenly...
I'm lying next to your
figure so sensual and sexually revealing.
This body of yours,
so worth any heart
to take for the stealing.
As your lips part
just for an excited
moment,
I watch, as the words
"I Love you" flow once again
across my pillow, just past my eyes
and ears and through my veins
for that split explosive and
chilling second.
To believe the moment,
I blink...
as you breathe
"I Love you" once more.

My heart rushes from my chest
and runs to catch these treasured
words and chart this endless guest,
of words I've waited so long to hear...
words that for so long... until forever,
I had always feared.

Taking in the moment...

though you're fading
to a blur from sight,
my thoughts of you,
Loving me...
breathing so deeply, run to find you
and meet you secretly in the night.

Suddenly back to now,
my tears of joyful sadness
roll gently down my face,
toward my lips,
that will catch your kiss,
when I really
find you again...
and I wonder when
that will come for me.
For "YOURS" is all
I ever really
wanted
to be.

Love, Randon 1988

I'm a FIRM believer in that,
Most all of us

Start out in life in our younger years
doing what we want to do...

Until one day we discover
what we were really MEANT to do.

And if we're really lucky, we find out
who we were really meant
to be with.

Everything is somewhere...

Even that perfect 'one-in-a-million' companion for you.

Just remember that nothing is perfect.

Nothing is perfect...

Nothing is forever...
so
How can perfect, forever and nothing be the same
thing?

I guess I'll never know.

Unless maybe when you told me that we were 'Perfect'
and that you would
Love me
'Forever'
was all 'nothing.'

That's it! I got it!
and that's all I got...
was it!

I'll Love you until before and after the day before and after the day after tomorrow... and I can truthfully guarantee you one thing in life.

There are absolutely
NO GUARANTEES.

But I will guarantee you that this is...

The End (not quite)

Oh! Now that I'm ready to leave...
you don't want me to go?

HA!

But...
If you're thinking about breaking up with someone who
has really been treating you badly and messing with
your mind...

And

You think you're gonna' be OK?... just as soon as you
get rid of them?

There's something you can do to really mess with their
mind.

When you make your request that you want to end
the relationship and they ask, "What's wrong don't you
Love me anymore?"

Just simply calmly respond by saying "YES",
While shaking your head
back and forth "NO"

Tell them...

"Sorry...
But if you had done things a little differently...
you wouldn't be apologizing now."
Say,
"Didn't you know that Love is never having to say
you're Sorry?"...

And remember,

Never do ANYTHING because or while you're very
angry.
Chill out and cool off first... but don't freeze up...or
you might regret it later.

Be sensitive...
But not senseless
and
If they ignore everything you've said about breaking up
and they say. "See ya' later." Just say,
"Don't threaten me!"
And if they say,"Call you later,"
say "Thanks for the warning!"

So once you're done with them and you're looking for someone new, just remember the Butterfly and you can't see where you're going...

while you've got your head in the clouds.

Rebounds can be really bad...

So... easy does it...

Think about what you're doing...

You may be setting yourself up for a big letdown.

Being HONEST with YOURSELF can be one of the hardest things you'll ever do...

So...I guess...

I can't Love you Forever,

maybe I'll just Love you for an eternity.

But that's a really long time too...

Especially when you're getting really close to The End.

Now... go fall in Love and be...
Happy.

Go...

Start somewhere...

At least get all the phone numbers you can
get
and If you want me to...
I'll call you later
and see how things went.

So remember if the phone <u>don't</u>
ring...
you'll know it's me.

And...

Even though I believe that
Love is the next best thing to Insanity.

I also know that...

In the End...

It's the only thing
that will keep us all sane.

Love, Randon Thorn

Forever

Printed in the United States
By Bookmasters